# Angelina Ballerina's Christmas Crafts

Illustrations by Helen Craig  Based on the text by Katharine Holabird

PLEASANT COMPANY PUBLICATIONS™

Published by Pleasant Company Publications
Illustrations © Helen Craig Limited
© 2003 Helen Craig Limited and Katharine Holabird

**Editorial Development** Sara Hunt
**Art Direction and Design** Lara Klipsch Elliott
**Stylist** Sarajane Lien
**Production** Cheryll Mellenthin, Lori Armstrong, and Cindy Hach
**Photographer** Radlund Photography and James Young

Visit our Web site at **www.americangirl.com** and Angelina's very own site at **www.angelinaballerina.com**

The Angelina Ballerina name and character and the dancing Angelina logo are trademarks of HIT Entertainment PLC, Katharine Holabird,
and Helen Craig Limited. ANGELINA is registered in the U.K. and Japan. The dancing Angelina logo is registered in the U.K.

Printed in China.

03 04 05 06 07 08 09  C&C  10 9 8 7 6 5 4 3 2 1
Library of Congress Cataloging-in-Publication Data available on request.

All the instructions in this book have been tested. Results from testing were incorporated into this book. Nonetheless,
all recommendations and suggestions are made without any guarantees on the part of Pleasant Company Publications.
Because of differing supplies, ingredients, conditions, and individual skills, the publisher disclaims liability for any
injuries, losses, or other damages that may result from using the information in this book.

Questions or comments? Call 1-800-845-0005, visit americangirl.com,
or write to American Girl, P.O. Box 620497, Middleton, WI 53562-0497.

*Special thanks to the little girls and their moms and dads who tested the crafts
and recipes in this book and gave us their valuable feedback:*

*Alyx Hach • Andie Hach • Katelin Hunt • Kelsey Hunt •
Taylor Jacobson • Alena Mears • Marissa Mears • Elise Powers*

# Get Ready...Get Set...Go!

*Here are some ideas for holiday baking and crafts for you to do with a parent. Each page shows an example of the finished product, but don't worry if yours looks different—the memory of doing something together is what makes each activity special.*

*—Angelina*

**Angelina says:**

1. Have a grown-up read through the instructions first and see what, if anything, can be done in advance and what materials are needed.

2. This helping hand symbol means that adult assistance is required. Of course, adult supervision is always recommended.

3. Do not use sharp knives or scissors unless a grown-up is helping you.

4. Never use an oven (even a microwave) or touch something hot by yourself.

5. Neatness counts! Wear a smock or apron, and tie back your hair. Remember to wash your hands before you cook and after you get messy from your hard work.

6. You're almost ready to begin! Now, be sure you have a clean, clear work surface, then gather all the materials you need before you get started!

# Table of Contents

*Start with Angelina's Christmas Countdown, then do one craft each day until Christmas. There are 26 crafts in all, and they're arranged in the order you'll need to do them to be ready for the big day. Or, pick and choose any craft or recipe to do anytime you like!*

# Craft Projects

*You can make a lot of projects with just a few basic items!*
*See the supplies box on each page to find out what else you might need.*
*All supplies are available at a craft supply store.*

**Beads and buttons**—a variety of buttons and beads in all shapes and sizes will be fun to use to decorate your creations. You'll also want a small supply of pipe cleaners, pom-poms, rhinestones, sequins, and wiggle eyes.

**Glue**—try to use tacky *craft glue* when gluing tiny parts or pieces. The stickiness helps little fingers position pieces and keep them in place. To thin craft glue, mix it with water and paint it on with a paintbrush. Special *fabric glue* is great for gluing fabric. *Glue sticks* provide neat and easy gluing for paper projects.

**Fabric, felt, and faux fur**—Use your imagination. Try different types of fabric.

**Glitter**—Pick an assortment of colors for lots of different looks. To conserve your glitter, hold your project over a paper plate when you sprinkle it. Then fold the plate and pour the excess glitter back into the container.

**Paint**—You'll want to use *acrylic paint* for many projects. *Fabric paint* or 3-D *puff paint* comes in squeeze bottles for simple styling.

**Ribbon, yarn, and thread**—Use whatever you have on hand!

**Scissors**—Use small round-tipped scissors. Have an adult cut cork or fabric.

**Tape**—Use masking tape, double-sided tape, or clear tape—whatever you have.

**Templates**—templates for several of Angelina's crafts are included at the back of the book. For other crafts, use cookie cutters to get the shapes you need.

# Cooking Projects

**Candy decorations, gumdrops, and edible glitter**—lots of sweet stuff can be found at grocery or baking supply stores. Or use whatever you have too much of at home!

**Cookie cutters**—use your favorite holiday cutters (about 2-inch shapes work best), or have a grown-up cut around some of the punch-out templates found in the back of this book.

**Measuring cups and spoons**—it's fun to measure and pour! Practice counting as you go.

**Wire rack**—use to cool cookies or dry ornaments. A paper towel or flat paper bag will work, too.

**Rolling pin, cookie sheets, and spatula**—these are important for making cookies and some nonedible projects, too.

**Ingredients**—you can substitute margarine for butter and baking chocolate for chocolate chips, and of course, make your own peanut butter cracker sandwiches or shred your own sharp Cheddar cheese (just like Mrs. Mouseling!).

**Plastic wrap, paper plates, wax paper, and zip-lock bags**—You can often substitute one for another, too. Wax paper makes a perfect surface for most of Angelina's projects. When you're done, just toss the mess!

# Angelina's Christmas Countdown

**Supplies:**
- Pretty paper (at least 2 colors)
- Dark crayon or number stickers (1–25)
- Glue stick or tape

How many days until Christmas?

*Angelina can't wait for Christmas—it seems so far away. But this pretty-colored paper chain helps her count the days.*

1 Cut out 25 strips of colored paper. With crayon or stickers, number the strips from 1 to 25. Shape the number 1 strip into a circle and glue the ends.

2 Link the number 2 color strip through the first, and glue it into a circle so you're making a chain. Continue with the remaining 23 strips.

3 Cut out a Christmas shape, and tape or glue the links to it (with the number 1 at the top).

4 Hang the paper chain in a special spot. Then, beginning on December 1, take one link from the bottom each day . . . until it's Christmas Day!

*Angelina decorates her tree with balls of glitter and sparkling beads!*

**Supplies:**
- Small Styrofoam ball
- Craft glue
- Glitter
- Beads
- Pipe cleaner

1 Paint Styrofoam ball with thinned glue and sprinkle with glitter over paper plate. Let dry. Re-glue and glitter any bare spots. Let dry again.

2 Poke beads into the ball for decorations and a pipe cleaner for a hanger.

10

# Picture Perfect Ornament

*Picture one of these precious
ornaments on your tree!*

**Supplies:**
- Mini craft box
- Acrylic paint
- Glitter
- Tiny pom-poms
- Small photo
- Pipe cleaner
- Craft glue
- Sequins

1. Paint a mini craft box and let dry. If desired, cover with thinned craft glue and sprinkle with glitter. Ask an adult to trim a photo to fit inside the box bottom.

2. Glue a small pom-pom inside the box, then glue on the picture. Use a pipe cleaner to make a hanger. Decorate a heart-shaped box with sequins and add a pom-pom to make it a tree.

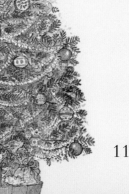

11

# Soap Snowmouse

**Supplies:**
- Ivory bar soap
- Peppercorns
- Twigs
- Ribbon

*Angelina absolutely loves snowy days at Miller's Pond. After the holidays, bring this snowmouse into the tub for some good, clean fun!*

1  Have a grown-up grate a bar of soap. Add a spoonful or two of water at a time, and stir until the mixture holds together but isn't too wet.

2  Make 3 soap balls for the body and head, and tiny soap balls for ears and a snout. Finish with peppercorn eyes and nose, twig arms, and a ribbon scarf.

# Snow Palace

**Supplies:**
- Sugar cubes
- Sugar cones
- Zip-lock sandwich bag
- Candy decorations

Cement frosting:
- 1 egg white
- ¼ teaspoon cream of tartar
- 1 cup powdered sugar
- Food coloring

1. Cement frosting: Have an adult beat egg white with cream of tartar till peaks form. Add powdered sugar and beat 5 minutes with electric mixer. Add food coloring.

2. Fill a sandwich bag with frosting. Snip off one corner of bag. Squeeze dots of frosting on sugar cubes to build your castle. Decorate cones for frosty trees.

14

Angelina and her friends helped Henry build a huge
Snow Palace for the ice skating show. You can create a
sweet fort with cement frosting and sugar cubes.

15

# Snowballs

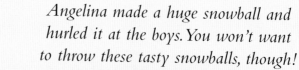

### Ingredients:

- 1 (12-ounce) package white chocolate chips
- 2 tablespoons vegetable shortening
- 1 box Ritz Bits peanut butter sandwiches
- White nonpareils

*Angelina made a huge snowball and hurled it at the boys. You won't want to throw these tasty snowballs, though!*

1  Have a grown-up melt chips and shortening in a microwave on medium-high for 1 minute. Stir. Microwave at additional 10-second intervals, stirring till smooth.

2  Dip cracker sandwiches into melted chocolate, then roll in nonpareils and place on wax paper until set.

# Cocoa Mix

**Supplies:**
- 1 cup sugar
- 2 cups instant nonfat dry milk powder
- ½ cup cocoa
- Jars, ribbon, fabric

*Mrs. Mouseling warmed up Angelina and her friends with steaming cocoa. Warm someone's heart with this delicious gift.*

1  Combine sugar, milk powder, and cocoa. Makes enough for 14 cups of hot cocoa.

2  Decorate jars with fabric and ribbons. Scoop mix into several airtight decorative jars.

3  If desired, attach handwritten instructions: For a cup of steaming cocoa, add 4 tablespoons mix to 1 cup of hot water. Stir well.

# Easy Cheese Crackers

*Angelina loves her mother's cheddar cheese pies more than anything in the world. These cheese crackers make a yummy bite-sized treat!*

## Ingredients:

- 2 sticks butter, softened
- 1 (8-ounce) bag shredded sharp Cheddar
- 2 cups flour
- 1 teaspoon salt
- 1½ cups crisp rice cereal

1 Mix butter and shredded cheese. Add flour and salt and mix well. Stir in cereal. Shape into small balls and place onto ungreased cookie sheet.

2 Press each cookie with a fork or your fingers until it is about ¼-inch thick. Have a grown-up bake at 400° for 12 to 15 minutes. Cool on rack.

# Angelina's Cottage

*Build a delicious miniature of Angelina's cozy cottage.*

**Supplies:**
- Graham crackers
- Cement frosting
- Zip-lock bag
- Small milk carton (clean and dry)
- Candy decorations
- Edible glitter

1 Spread cement frosting (page 14) onto 4 graham cracker squares. Press one square onto each side of the milk carton. Decorate with candy and frosting.

2 Frost 2 graham crackers and build a roof. To create the look of newly fallen snow, frost the rooftop and sprinkle with edible glitter.

# Cozy Bookmarks

*Miss Lilly would love one of these special bookmarks. Make one—or two—for your teacher, too!*

**Supplies:**
- Felt (any color)
- Mitten and stocking templates (page 45)
- Spring curl hair clip
- Craft glue
- Glitter, stickers, fabric paint, and micro beads

1 Trace the template 4 times onto felt, and have a grown-up cut out shapes. On 2 of the cutouts, trim the top edge slightly. Use one of each size for each side of the clip.

2 Open the clip. For each side, make a sandwich around the clip with a small cutout on the inside and a large one on the outside. Glue together. Let dry. Decorate as desired.

# Gingerboy Magnet

**Supplies:**
- Thin, fine-grade corkboard
- Gingerboy template (page 45)
- Markers
- Craft glue
- Buttons
- Yarn and ribbon
- Magnet

*Grandma and Grandpa will be excited to see this adorable magnet under the tree.*

1 Trace the template onto flattened corkboard and have a grown-up cut out the shape.

2 Draw eyes and mouth with markers. Decorate with glue, buttons, ribbon, and yarn. Glue a magnet to the back.

# Shining Star Ornaments

*Angelina is the star of the ice skating show!*

**Supplies:**
- 1 cup cornstarch
- 2 cups baking soda
- 1½ cups water
- Paper clips
- Craft glue
- Fabric paint
- Glitter
- Rhinestones
- Ribbon

1    Mix cornstarch and baking soda in a large pot. Add water. Stir until smooth. Cover and have a grown-up cook over medium heat till mixture is like mashed potatoes.

2    Turn onto a counter and cover with a damp cloth. When cool enough to handle, knead with cornstarch till smooth. Roll and cut with cookie cutters.

3  Insert an opened paper clip into the top edge of each shape. Have a grown-up bake them on a cookie sheet at 275° until hard, about 20 minutes.

4  When cool, decorate with glue and glitter, fabric paint, and rhinestones. Tie a pretty ribbon through the paper clip loop to hang.

# Sweet Spice Ornaments

## Supplies:

- One 4-ounce can ground cinnamon
- ¾ cup applesauce
- 2 tablespoons Elmer's glue
- 1 tablespoon each nutmeg, cloves (optional)
- Drinking straw

*These decorations smell so sweet . . . but remember, they're not to eat!*

1 Combine all ingredients. Mix with hands for 2 to 3 minutes, until smooth. Divide dough into 4 equal portions.

2 Roll each portion out between sheets of wax paper to ¼-inch thick.

3 Cut with cookie cutters, using a straw to make a hole in the top center of each shape.

24

4 Place on wax paper and let dry at room temperature for several days. For even drying and to prevent curling, flip the shapes once each day.

5 If desired, use fabric paint or permanent markers to decorate.

6 Use finished shapes as ornaments or gift tags. Tie ribbon through the holes to hang or attach to gifts.

*Fast and easy . . .
with sparkly results!*

**Supplies:**
- Plastic wrap or wax paper
- Paper plate
- Craft glue
- Lots of glitter

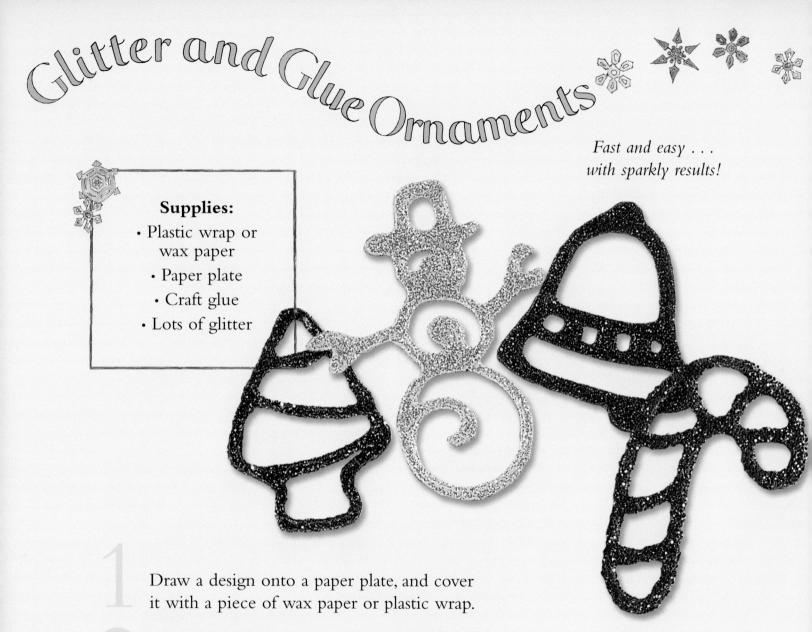

**1** Draw a design onto a paper plate, and cover it with a piece of wax paper or plastic wrap.

**2** Trace the image with a thick line of glue onto the wax paper or plastic wrap. Sprinkle with lots of glitter and let dry. Peel from paper and hang.

# Nifty Noodle Snowflakes

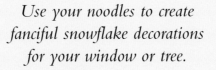

*Use your noodles to create fanciful snowflake decorations for your window or tree.*

**Supplies:**
- Pasta (rotini, wagon wheel, fettucine)
- Craft glue
- Acrylic paints
- Shimmery acrylic glaze

1  Arrange pasta into snowflake shapes. Glue shapes together with tacky craft glue and let dry.

2  Paint with acrylic paints, and, if desired, accent with shimmery glaze. Let dry. Have an adult hang with filament or string.

27

# Tiny Tree

*Decorate a pint-sized version of Angelina's holiday tree.*

**Supplies:**
- Pinecone
- Small clay pot
- Acrylic paints
- Pipe cleaner
- Craft glue
- Sequins or mini pom-poms

1   Paint pinecone and clay pot with acrylic paint. Let dry. Have an adult help you wrap a pipe cleaner around as a garland. Line inner rim of the pot with glue and set pinecone inside.

2   Use dots of glue to attach sequins or mini pom-poms for ornaments. Top with a sequin star.

**Supplies:**
- Stale bread
- Drinking straw
- Yarn
- Peanut butter
- Mixed birdseed
- Currants

*Hang some ornaments outside, too! The birds will thank you.*

1. Cut shapes out of slices of stale bread with cookie cutters. Use a straw to make a hanging hole in each shape. Thread yarn through each hole.

2. Spread peanut butter onto shapes, and sprinkle with birdseed. Decorate with sunflower seeds and currants. Let bread dry, then hang outside for the birds.

29

# Bend 'n Bead Tree

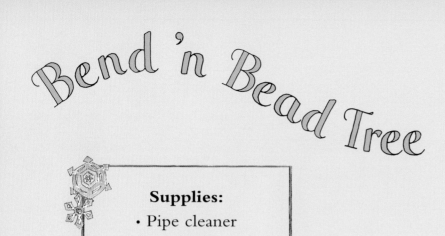

*Angelina remembers that Christmas is a time for giving when she brings a tree and goodies to Mr. Bell.*

**Supplies:**
- Pipe cleaner
- Beads
- Star-shaped bead or button

**1** String beads along a pipe cleaner. Add a star bead to one end. Bend the pipe cleaner around each end bead to hold it in place.

**2** Form the beaded pipe cleaner into a tree shape.

# Gumdrop Wreath

*Make a yummy, gummy wreath for a decoration or snack.*

**Supplies:**
- 7 mint-leaf gumdrops
- 3 red gumdrops
- 3 white gumdrops
- Colored toothpicks, broken in half
- Ribbons

1 Use green toothpick pieces to connect green gumdrops in a wreath shape.

2 Have an adult cut red and white gumdrops in half— eat the bottom halves! Use red and white toothpick pieces to add red and white gumdrop holly berries.

3 Use pieces of silver and gold ribbon to finish with a bow.

# Candycane Mouse

**Supplies:**
- White felt or faux fur
- White or pink felt
- Candy cane
- Craft glue
- Wiggle eyes
- Small gray pom pom
- Ribbon
- Templates (page 47)

*Not a creature was stirring . . .*

1. Trace the templates and have a grown-up cut out mouse body and ears. Cut small slits where indicated and slide the ears into place.

2. Slide the candy cane into the slit. Secure with craft glue. Glue on a pom-pom nose and wiggle eyes, and tie a bow around the tail.

# Quiet Little Mouse

*. . . not even a mouse!*

**Supplies:**
- Small medicine cup or nutshell (half)
- Acrylic paints
- Craft glue
- Small, medium, and large pom-poms
- Micro beads
- Pipe cleaner
- Felt, ribbon

1 Paint a medicine cup or nutshell. Let dry. Glue one large pom-pom inside, then a medium one for a head, and two small ones for ears.

2 Glue on micro bead features and a bent pipe cleaner tail. Finish with a felt handle for a teacup or a pink ribbon for the nutshell. Glue into place. Let dry.

33

# Angelina's Crown

**Supplies:**
- 8½-by-11-inch glittery craft paper
- Template (page 47)
- Craft glue
- Double-sided tape
- Pipe cleaners
- Beads and rhinestones

1  Trace the template (page 47) onto glittery craft paper and have a grown-up cut out, leaving a 2-inch-wide strip. Add rhinestones with craft glue.

2  Tape 3 bent pipe cleaners and 3 pipe cleaners with beaded ends to back side of crown, as shown. Attach leftover paper strip with tape to fit.

# ...and Fairy Wand

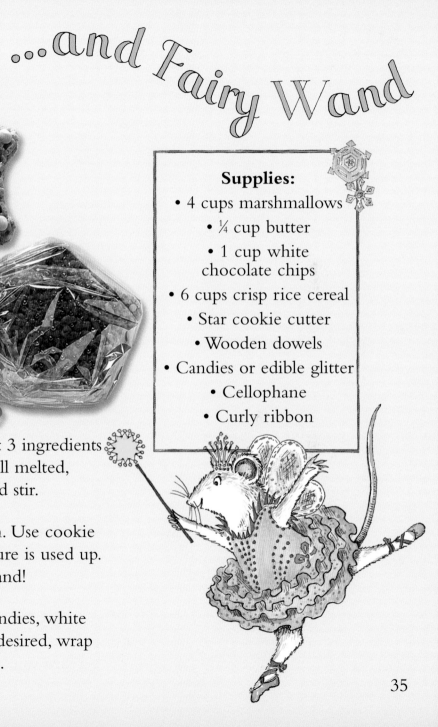

*On the night of her first performance, Angelina waited backstage with her crown on and her wand ready . . .*

**Supplies:**
- 4 cups marshmallows
- ¼ cup butter
- 1 cup white chocolate chips
- 6 cups crisp rice cereal
- Star cookie cutter
- Wooden dowels
- Candies or edible glitter
- Cellophane
- Curly ribbon

1. Have a grown-up microwave first 3 ingredients on high for 3 to 3½ minutes or till melted, stirring after 2 minutes. Add cereal and stir.

2. Press mixture into lightly greased pan. Use cookie cutters to make large stars until mixture is used up. Insert a dowel to make each star a wand!

3. Cool for one hour. Decorate with candies, white chocolate chips, and edible glitter. If desired, wrap in cellophane, then add curly ribbons.

# The Nutcracker Suite

*Put on your own little performance of* **The Nutcracker!**

**Supplies:**
- Wooden clothespin
- Acrylic paints
- Pipe cleaners
- Wide wire-edged ribbon
- Tacky craft glue
- Small pom-poms
- Colored pearl beads
- Gold braid trim

1 Paint clothespin. Let dry. Wrap one pipe cleaner around upper body, bend ends for arms. Wrap lower body with another pipe cleaner, tucking in edges.

2 Have a grown-up cut a section of ribbon. On one edge, pull wires at each end to gather fabric in the middle. Wrap the ribbon around upper clothespin section and twist together in back to secure.

3 Glue on pom-poms and beads to make a face and ears, and a snip of gold braid for a crown. If desired, paint ballet slippers. Let dry.

# Mrs. Mouseling's Christmas Biscuits

*Make these biscuits for your family and friends. The recipe is so simple, you can almost make them by yourself!*

## Ingredients:
- 1 stick chilled butter
- ¾ cup flour
- ¼ cup sugar
- 1 teaspoon vanilla
- Colored sugars

1 Grease 2 cookie sheets with butter or margarine. Cut butter into small pieces in a bowl. Add flour and sugar.

2 Mix together with a fork and then with your fingers, till dough is crumbly.

3 Add vanilla and mix well with a fork. Then gently squeeze the mixture into a ball.

4 Sprinkle flour onto a countertop and knead the dough into a smooth, firm ball. Roll with a floured rolling pin till dough is about ¼-inch thick.

5 Cut shapes with cookie cutters. Place shapes onto greased cookie sheets and decorate with colored sugar.

6 Have a grown-up bake cookies for 20 minutes or till they're light golden. Cool for 5 minutes on the cookie sheet before moving to a wire rack to cool.

**Supplies:**
- Cardboard rolls
- Crepe paper
- Clear tape
- Curling ribbon
- Small surprises

1 For each cracker, roll a 4 ½-inch cardboard tube (such as a toilet paper roll) in 2 layers of crepe paper. Leave 3 inches of paper at each end. Tape the middle.

2 Gather paper at one end and tie with ribbon. Pour confetti, small toys, or treats into the other end, and tie with ribbon. When it's time to celebrate, pop open by tugging at both ends.

*Christmas crackers are a special holiday tradition in Angelina's village.*
*Make some to add fun to your Christmas or New Year's celebration.*

# Snowy Day Fun

*The weather outside might be frightful, but the fun that
a snowy day brings can really be delightful! You don't even have
to bundle up in a snowsuit to enjoy some of these winter fun ideas.*

**Ice cream snow**

Blend 1 cup half-and-half, ½ cup sugar, and 1 teaspoon vanilla in
a big bowl. Have an adult add fresh, clean snow until mixture is
absorbed. A tasty treat!

**Play in the snow—inside!**

Bring in a big bowl of clean, fluffy snow. Dump it onto
a cookie sheet and get out some sandbox toys, little cars, and
mini people. Have a ball inside in the snow—while it lasts!

**Unfold an indoor blizzard!**

Fold clean coffee filters into fourths, and cut out teeny, tiny shapes along
the edges to make snowflakes. Tint the flakes by dipping them in cups
of colored water. String them onto thread for a pretty (easy!) garland.

**Paint your snowscape a rainbow of bright colors**

For some colorful outdoor fun, fill several squirt bottles with water,
add a few squirts of a different food color to each, and shake well.

# ❄ ❄Tips for Parents❄ ❄

*Try these ways to share your values—and
time—with your children this holiday season.*

**Create a few simple family traditions.**
Traditions don't have to be elaborate. They can be something simple, like decorating cookies, making ornaments, or drinking hot cocoa—anything a child can count on doing every year.

The security of having a routine during the holidays, just like at every other time of year, is comforting to small children.

**Minimize the hoopla.**
Wait until early to mid-December to start involving your children in holiday preparations. Also, try to plan something special for children to look forward to *after* Christmas Day, such as going to see *The Nutcracker*, ice-skating as a family, or enjoying a special New Year's dinner. This takes the focus off the anticipation of gifts, and spreads the excitement to other activities.

**Teach your child the joy of giving.**
By helping your child make simple gifts for others, you are giving her some of the greatest gifts of all—the feeling of satisfaction and a valuable lesson in sharing goodwill.

Punch out the templates on the following pages and put them somewhere for safekeeping.

Attach the gift tags on the following pages to your creations to make special gifts for family and friends. Use a sticker to attach each gift tag, or punch a hole in the tag and tie with ribbon. Decorate your holiday crafts or packages with the extra snowflake stickers.

Aluminum foil makes a sparkly, kid-friendly gift wrap. Take a large piece of foil and use it to wrap gifts—all by yourself! You can tuck corners into place and seal with some tape. For a beautiful finish, add some of Angelina's snowflake stickers and a pretty bow!

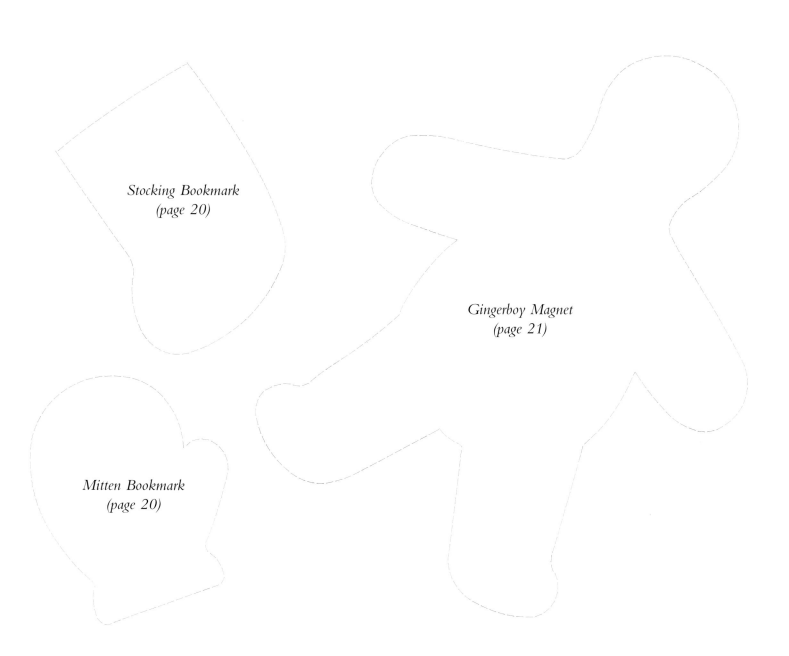

*Stocking Bookmark*
*(page 20)*

*Gingerboy Magnet*
*(page 21)*

*Mitten Bookmark*
*(page 20)*

*Angelina's Crown*
*(page 34)*

*Candycane Mouse Body*
*(page 32)*

*Candycane Mouse Ears*

To: _____

From: _____

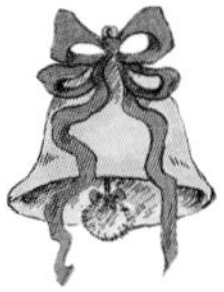

To: _____

From: _____

To: _____

From: _____

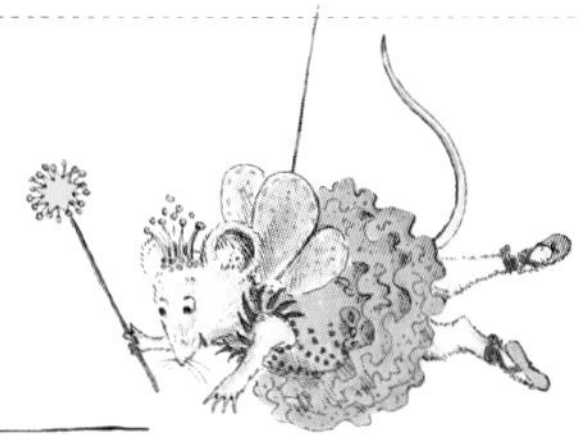

To: _____

From: _____

To: _____

From: _____

To: _____

From: _____

To: _____

From: _____

To: _____

From: _____

To: _____
From: _____

To: _____
From: _____

To: _____
From: _____

To: _____
From: _____

To: _____
From: _____

To: _____
From: _____

To: _____
From: _____

To: _____
From: _____